A Big Fish Story
The Story of Jonah

We are grateful to the following team of authors for their contributions to *God Loves Me,* a Bible story program for young children. This Bible story, one of a series of fifty-two, was written by Patricia L. Nederveld, managing editor for CRC Publications. Suggestions for using this book were developed by Jesslyn DeBoer, a freelance author from Grand Rapids, Michigan. Yvonne Van Ee, an early childhood educator, served as project consultant and wrote *God Loves Me,* the program guide that accompanies this series of Bible storybooks.

Nederveld has served as a consultant to Title I early childhood programs in Colorado. She has extensive experience as a writer, teacher, and consultant for federally funded preschool, kindergarten, and early childhood programs in Colorado, Texas, Michigan, Florida, Missouri, and Washington, using the *High/Scope* Education Research Foundation curriculum. In addition to writing the *Bible Footprints* church curriculum for four- and five-year-olds, Nederveld edited the revised *Threes* curriculum and the first edition of preschool through second grade materials for the *LiFE* curriculum, all published by CRC Publications.

DeBoer has served as a church preschool leader and as coauthor of the preschool-kindergarten materials for the *LiFE* curriculum published by CRC Publications. She has also written K-6 science and health curriculum for Christian Schools International, Grand Rapids, Michigan, and inspirational gift books for Zondervan Publishing House.

Van Ee is a professor and early childhood program advisor in the Education Department at Calvin College, Grand Rapids, Michigan. She has served as curriculum author and consultant for Christian Schools International and wrote the original *Story Hour* organization manual and curriculum materials for fours and fives.

Photo on page 5: Peter Correz/Tony Stone Images; photo on page 20: Donna Day/Tony Stone Images.

Library of Congress Cataloging-in-Publication Data

Nederveld, Patricia L., 1944-
    A big fish story: the story of Jonah/Patricia L. Nederveld.
        p. cm. — (God loves me; bk. 22)
    Summary: Retells the story of Jonah, who refused to obey God and is
rescued from a stormy sea by a whale. Includes follow-up activities.
    ISBN 1-56212-291-6
    1. Elisha (Biblical prophet)—Juvenile literature. 2. Bible stories, English
—O.T. Jonah. 3. Bible games and puzzles. [1. Elisha (Biblical prophet).
2. Bible stories—O.T.] I. Title. II. Series: Nederveld, Patricia L., 1944-
God loves me; bk. 22.
BS580.J55N43 1998
224'.9209505—dc21   97-32477
                                                              CIP
                                                              AC

10 9 8 7 6 5 4 3 2 1

A Big Fish Story
The Story of Jonah

PATRICIA L. NEDERVELD

ILLUSTRATIONS BY LISA WORKMAN

CRC Publications
Grand Rapids, Michigan

This is a story from God's book, the Bible.

It's for say name(s) of your child(ren). It's for me too!

Jonah 1-3

Hello there! My name is Jonah. Have I got a big fish story to tell you! It all began when God gave me a job to do . . .

"Go to Nineveh," God said. "I don't like the bad things I see people doing there. Tell them to stop their bad ways and obey me!"

Well, I should have obeyed God right away. But I didn't want to go to Nineveh. Not one bit! So instead I climbed on a ship that was going the other way. And, just to make sure God couldn't find me, I curled up in a hiding place at the bottom of the ship.

But that didn't work at all! God knew exactly where I was. Before long, God sent a great storm. The wind howled and waves crashed over our ship. Everyone was frightened!

"Oops! This is my fault!" I told everyone. "If you throw me into the water, God will stop the storm."

The water was deep and dark—but God could see me. God knew exactly where I was. And, just in time, God sent a giant fish to rescue me!

Do you think God can see me sitting here in the tummy of the fish? Why, of course! Now I know that God is with us everywhere!

And now I know that God *really* wants me to go to Nineveh. But first I have to get out of this fish . . .

Well, here I am—it feels good to be back on land again. There's only one thing for me to do now—obey God.

This time I'm going straight to Nineveh.
Everyone there needs to know . . .

that God is with
us everywhere.
And obeying God
is the very best
way to live.

I wonder if you know that God is with you wherever you are . . .

Dear God, thank you for always knowing where we are. We're glad you are with us right now! Amen.

Suggestions for Follow-up

Opening

Take a few minutes to gather as a group with your children. Go around the circle, naming each child. When everyone has been mentioned, ask your little ones if they know who else is with you. Remind them that God is always with us—at home, at church—everywhere!

Celebrate God's presence as you encourage children to mimic these words and actions:

> God is here with us! Hurray! (clap twice)
> Thank you, God for this fine day. (fold hands in prayer)
> Hurray, Hurray! (clap twice and then twice again)

Learning Through Play

Learning through play is the best way! The following activity suggestions are meant to help you provide props and experiences that will invite the children to play their way into the Scripture story and its simple truth. Try to provide plenty of time for the children to choose their own activities and to play individually. Use group activities sparingly—little ones learn most comfortably with a minimum of structure.

1. Cover a table with a plastic shower curtain liner, and protect the floor with newspaper or plastic. Prepare a package of instant vanilla pudding (add a drop or two of blue food coloring with the milk). Provide paint shirts, and invite your little ones to finger paint with a small amount of pudding. Talk about the big waves that crashed over Jonah's ship, and show the children how to paint waves on the table liner. Older children may want to add a boat and a big fish to the scene.

2. Provide dress-up clothes and accessories to help children think about places people go. You might add sturdy boxes for cars or buses children can drive or ride. Mommies and Daddies go to work, to the store, or to the library with their children. Firefighters go to put out fires, teachers go to school, families go to the zoo and to church. Look for opportunities to remind the children that God is with us *everywhere* we go.

3. Set up a water table with dishpans or an infant bathtub. Add plastic boats and toy people. You can use a see-through plastic bottle for the big fish or a plastic fish bank. Make sure the bottle or bank is large enough to hold one of the toy people. Play with the children, acting out and retelling the story of Jonah. Hide Jonah on the ship, stir the water to create the storm, throw Jonah overboard, hide Jonah in the big fish, and then bring him out again. Remind your little ones that God knew where Jonah was. God was with Jonah everywhere!

4. Invite one or more children to play "Hide Jonah" with you. Use a small wooden toy person for Jonah. Tell your little ones that this person's name is Jonah and that sometimes he likes to hide. Place the toy in a fairly obvious place on a shelf or table. You can choose more difficult hiding places, and let the children take

turns helping you hide Jonah. Remind them that God always knew where Jonah was, and God always knows where we are too.

5. Invite children to take turns being Jonah. Jonah can hide while the other children cover their eyes with their hands. As you hunt for Jonah, sing this song (tune: "Where Is Thumbkin?"):

> *Where is Jonah?*
> *Where is Jonah?*
> *Here he is.*
> *Here he is.*
> *I'm so glad God sees you.*
> *I'm so glad God sees you.*
> *God loves you.*

You can insert each child's name in the song in place of Jonah's. Take one or two children by the hand as you begin to sing and search for the child you've named. Or you may want to use this game as a way to gather up the children for closing time—join hands and add one child at a time to your string of children as you weave through the room.

6. To help your little ones remember what God wanted Jonah—and all of us—to do, sing this chorus to the refrain of "Jesus Loves Me" (Songs Section, *God Loves Me* program guide)

> *Hey, Jonah, Jonah!*
> *Hey, Jonah, Jonah!*
> *Hey, Jonah, Jonah!*
> *You should obey the Lord.*

> *Lord, we'll obey you!*
> *Lord, we'll obey you!*
> *Lord, we'll obey you!*
> *We will obey the Lord.*

Closing
Close your time together with the prayer on page 21. Take a moment as the children leave to assure them that God is with them wherever they go.

At Home
Situations such as moving or traveling can produce anxiety and insecurity in young children. When familiar surroundings and routines are disrupted, your child may need an extra measure of your care and attention. Pack a travel bag for your child with a favorite Bible storybook, a cassette of familiar songs, and pictures of happy times. Reassure your little one that God is with your family wherever you go. When life is more routine, capture every opportunity to build your child's trust in God's ever-caring presence. As you're leaving for work or an evening out, when bringing your child to a care provider, or when piling into the car for a family outing, point out that God is with you. Encourage your child to add, "Hurray! Hurray!"

Old Testament Stories

Blue and Green and Purple Too! *The Story of God's Colorful World*

It's a Noisy Place! *The Story of the First Creatures*

Adam and Eve *The Story of the First Man and Woman*

Take Good Care of My World! *The Story of Adam and Eve in the Garden*

A Very Sad Day *The Story of Adam and Eve's Disobedience*

A Rainy, Rainy Day *The Story of Noah*

Count the Stars! *The Story of God's Promise to Abraham and Sarah*

A Girl Named Rebekah *The Story of God's Answer to Abraham*

Two Coats for Joseph *The Story of Young Joseph*

Plenty to Eat *The Story of Joseph and His Brothers*

Safe in a Basket *The Story of Baby Moses*

I'll Do It! *The Story of Moses and the Burning Bush*

Safe at Last! *The Story of Moses and the Red Sea*

What Is It? *The Story of Manna in the Desert*

A Tall Wall *The Story of Jericho*

A Baby for Hannah *The Story of an Answered Prayer*

Samuel! Samuel! *The Story of God's Call to Samuel*

Lions and Bears! *The Story of David the Shepherd Boy*

David and the Giant *The Story of David and Goliath*

A Little Jar of Oil *The Story of Elisha and the Widow*

One, Two, Three, Four, Five, Six, Seven! *The Story of Elisha and Naaman*

A Big Fish Story *The Story of Jonah*

Lions, Lions! *The Story of Daniel*

New Testament Stories

Jesus Is Born! *The Story of Christmas*

Good News! *The Story of the Shepherds*

An Amazing Star! *The Story of the Wise Men*

Waiting, Waiting, Waiting! *The Story of Simeon and Anna*

Who Is This Child? *The Story of Jesus in the Temple*

Follow Me! *The Story of Jesus and His Twelve Helpers*

The Greatest Gift *The Story of Jesus and the Woman at the Well*

A Father's Wish *The Story of Jesus and a Little Boy*

Just Believe! *The Story of Jesus and a Little Girl*

Get Up and Walk! *The Story of Jesus and a Man Who Couldn't Walk*

A Little Lunch *The Story of Jesus and a Hungry Crowd*

A Scary Storm *The Story of Jesus and a Stormy Sea*

Thank You, Jesus! *The Story of Jesus and One Thankful Man*

A Wonderful Sight! *The Story of Jesus and a Man Who Couldn't See*

A Better Thing to Do *The Story of Jesus and Mary and Martha*

A Lost Lamb *The Story of the Good Shepherd*

Come to Me! *The Story of Jesus and the Children*

Have a Great Day! *The Story of Jesus and Zacchaeus*

I Love You, Jesus! *The Story of Mary's Gift to Jesus*

Hosanna! *The Story of Palm Sunday*

The Best Day Ever! *The Story of Easter*

Goodbye—for Now *The Story of Jesus' Return to Heaven*

A Prayer for Peter *The Story of Peter in Prison*

Sad Day, Happy Day! *The Story of Peter and Dorcas*

A New Friend *The Story of Paul's Conversion*

Over the Wall *The Story of Paul's Escape in a Basket*

A Song in the Night *The Story of Paul and Silas in Prison*

A Ride in the Night *The Story of Paul's Escape on Horseback*

The Shipwreck *The Story of Paul's Rescue at Sea*

Holiday Stories

Selected stories from the New Testament to help you celebrate the Christian year

Jesus Is Born! *The Story of Christmas*

Good News! *The Story of the Shepherds*

An Amazing Star! *The Story of the Wise Men*

Hosanna! *The Story of Palm Sunday*

The Best Day Ever! *The Story of Easter*

Goodbye—for Now *The Story of Jesus' Return to Heaven*

These fifty-two books are the heart of *God Loves Me*, a Bible story program designed for young children. Individual books (or the entire set) and the accompanying program guide *God Loves Me* are available from CRC Publications (1-800-333-8300).